PEGASUS ENCYCLOPEDIA LIBRARY

Food and Nutrition
FOOD

Edited by: Pallabi B. Tomar, Hitesh Iplani
Managing editor: Tapasi De
Designed by: Vijesh Chahal, Anil Kumar, Rohit Kumar
Illustrated by: Suman S. Roy, Tanoy Choudhury
Colouring done by: Vinay Kumar, Kiran Kumari & Pradeep Kumar

CONTENTS

What is food? 3

Types of food 4

Food sources 8

Food chain 10

Food production through agriculture 12

Taste of food 14

Methods of preparing food 17

Food trade 23

Food poverty 24

Food allergy and intolerance 26

Food safety methods 29

Test Your Memory 31

Index 32

What is food?

Food is any substance normally eaten or drunk by living organisms. The term food also includes liquid drinks. Food is the main source of energy and of nutrition for animals and man and is usually of animal or plant origin.

The study of food is called **food science**. Historically, people obtained food from hunting and gathering, farming, ranching, and fishing, known as agriculture. Today, most of the food energy consumed by the world population is supplied by the food industry operated by multinational corporations using intensive farming and industrial agriculture methods.

Food safety and food security are monitored by agencies such as the International Association for Food Protection, World Resources Institute, World Food Programme, Food and Agriculture Organization and International Food Information Council. They address issues such as sustainability, biological diversity, climate change, nutritional economics, population growth, water supply and access to food.

Astonishing fact

During the Alaskan Klondike gold rush (1897-1898), potatoes were practically worth their weight in gold. Potatoes were so valued for their vitamin C content that miners traded gold for potatoes!

Types of food

Fast food

Fast food is any food that is quick, convenient and usually inexpensive. You can buy fast food just about anywhere that sells food and snacks. Vending machines, drive-through restaurants and 24 hour convenience stores are probably the most common places to find fast food. However, fast food is inexpensive because it is usually made with cheaper ingredients such as high fat meat, refined grains and added sugar and fats, instead of nutritious foods such as lean meats, fresh fruits and vegetables.

Fast-food outlets are take-away or take-out providers, often with a 'drive-thru' service which allows customers to order and pick up food from their cars; but most of them also have a seating area in which customers can eat the food on the premises.

Nearly from its inception, fast food has been designed to be eaten 'on the go' and often does not require traditional dominant cutlery. Common menu items at fast food outlets include fish and chips, sandwiches, pitas, hamburgers, fried chicken, French fries, chicken nuggets, tacos, pizza and ice cream.

Fortune cookies were invented in 1916 by George Jung, a Los Angeles noodle maker.

Types of food

Junk food

Any food that has poor nutritional value is considered unhealthy maybe called a junk food. A food that is high in fat, sodium and sugar is known as a junk food. Junk food is easy to carry, purchase and consume. Generally, a junk food is given a very attractive appearance by adding food additives and colours to enhance flavour, texture, appearance and increasing long self life.

A junk food has little enzyme producing vitamins and minerals and contains high level of calories. When we eat these empty calorie foods, the body is required to produce its own enzymes to convert these empty calories into usable energy. This is not desired as these enzyme producing functions in our body should be reserved for the performance of vital metabolic reactions.

Since junk food is high in fats and sugars, it is responsible for obesity, dental cavities, Type 2 diabetes and heart diseases.

Foods which fall under junk food vary depending on a number of factors. Snack foods like chips, candies and so forth are generally universally agreed upon as junk food, and some people also include fast food like hamburgers, pizza and fries into the junk food category.

> **McDonald's fast food chains employ over 1.5 million people around the world.**

Whole foods

Whole foods are foods that are as close to their natural or original states as possible. This means they have not been processed or refined. It also means they are free of additives, such as colourings and preservatives and have not been modified.

Fruits and vegetables are great examples of whole foods. They are unprocessed, unrefined and can be eaten without any additives or modifications. Nuts, seeds, beans, lentils and peas also make the grade. Milk and eggs can be included in this category, as can meats, poultry and fish.

One reason to choose whole foods over their processed counterparts is nutritional intake. Often, as a result of processing, important vitamins and minerals are lost and the food may become less healthy. Even things like fibre and water can be diminished through processing and refinement making the food significantly less useful for the body.

Another benefit whole foods offer over processed choices is the lack of added sugar and sodium. Obesity is a problem in some countries, a fact that is probably influenced by the added sugars in the foods we eat. Likewise, excess sodium can contribute to health problems such as high blood pressure and many processed foods are high in sodium.

Cutting onions releases a gas which causes a stinging sensation when it comes into contact with your eyes. Your body produces tears to dilute the irritant and remove it from your eyes.

Organic food

Organic food refers to the food items that are produced, processed and packaged without using chemicals. Organic food is increasingly becoming popular due to its perceived health benefits over conventional food. The industry is growing rapidly since the past five years and has caught the attention of farmers, manufacturers and above all, consumers.

The organic revolution is a global phenomenon witnessed in every part of the world including US, Canada, Mexico, Austria, Denmark, Finland, France, Germany, Italy, The Netherlands, Spain, Sweden, Switzerland, UK, Hungary, Poland, Australia, New Zealand, China, India, Japan, Malaysia,

> **Rice is the staple food of more than one-half of the world's population.**

Singapore, Thailand, Turkey, Argentina, Brazil, Chile and South Africa. These regions are important production as well as demand centres.

Popular organic food items include organic tea, organic coffee, organic wine, organic meat, organic beef, organic milk, organic honey, organic vegetables, organic fruits, organic rice, organic corn, organic herbs, organic essential oils, organic coconut oil and organic olive oil.

Food sources

Almost all foods are of plant or animal origin. Cereal grain is a staple food that provides more food energy worldwide than any other type of crop. Maize, wheat and rice together account for 87 per cent of all grain production worldwide. Other foods not from animal or plant sources include various edible fungi, especially mushrooms. Fungi and bacteria are used in the preparation of fermented and pickled foods such as leavened bread, alcoholic drinks, cheese, pickles and yogurt.

From plants

- Grasses and their grains, including barley, cereals, couscous, corn or maize, oats, rice, rye, sugarcane, wheat, etc
- Fruits
- Herbs
- Legumes, including beans, peas, lentils, etc
- Nuts
- Seeds
- Spices
- Vegetables

Saffron, made from the dried stamens of cultivated crocus flowers is the most expensive cooking spice.

Food sources

From animals

- Dairy products, including milk
- Eggs
- Insects, including honey
- Meat, including beef, goat, horse, kangaroo, lamb, mutton, pork, veal
- Poultry, including chicken, turkey, duck, goose, pigeon or dove, ostrich, emu, guinea fowl, pheasant, quail
- Seafood, including finfish such as salmon and tilapia, and shellfish such as mollusks and crustaceans
- Snails

Astonishing fact

The colour of a chilli is no indication of its spiciness, but size usually matters; the smaller, the hotter it is.

From neither animals or plants

- Salt
- Mushrooms
- Water, including mineral water and spring water

Spring water

Food chain

Every plant and animal species, no matter how big or small, depends to some extent on another plant or animal species for its survival. It could be bees taking pollen from a flower, photosynthesis of plants, deer eating shrub leaves or lions eating the deer.

A food chain shows how energy is transferred from one living organism to another via food. It is important for us to understand how the food chain works so that we know what are the important living organisms that make up the food chain and how the ecology is balanced.

A food chain describes how energy and nutrients move through an ecosystem. At the basic level there are plants that produce the energy, then it moves up to higher-level organisms like herbivores. After that when carnivores eat the herbivores, energy is transferred from one to the other.

In the food chain, energy is transferred from one living organism through another in the form of food. There are primary producers, primary consumers, secondary consumers and decomposers- all part of the food chain.

When honey is swallowed, it enters the blood stream within a period of 20 minutes.

Food chain

Herbivores

Producers are always the first link in a food chain. Producers are plants and are capable of making their own food through the process of photosynthesis. Grass is an example of a producer.

Primary consumers are the next link in a food chain. Herbivores or plant eaters are the first consumer of the energy produced by plants. A rabbit is a prime example of a primary consumer.

Secondary consumers are carnivores or meat eaters and are the third link in the food chain. They obtain energy by eating herbivores. An example of a secondary consumer is a fox. A secondary consumer can also be an omnivore, an animal that consumes plants and animals.

Decomposers are the final link in the food chain. A decomposer breaks down dead plants and animals, so they can become food for plants. Worms are decomposers.

Astonishing fact

Three quarters of fish caught are eaten. The rest is used to make things such as glue, soap, margarine and fertilizer.

This interdependence of the populations within a food chain helps to maintain the balance of plant and animal populations within a community. For example, when there are too many giraffes, there will be insufficient trees and shrubs for all of them to eat. Many giraffes will starve and die. Fewer giraffes means more time for the trees and shrubs to grow to maturity and multiply. Fewer giraffes also mean less food is available for the lions to eat and some lions will starve to death. When there are fewer lions, the giraffe population will increase.

Omnivore

Carnivore

Food production through agriculture

Civilization began with agriculture, our nomadic ancestors settled once they began to grow their own food.

Agriculture refers to the production of goods through growing of plants, animals and other life forms on land. As of 2006, 45 per cent of the world's population is employed in agriculture.

However, the relative significance of farming has dropped since the beginning of industrialization. Even though agriculture employs one-third of the world's population, agricultural produce accounts for less than 5 per cent of the gross world product.

Agriculture is a very important activity for the survival of human beings on this Earth. This is clearly reflected in the very basic fact that agriculture is one of the oldest activities of humankind. The term 'agriculture' includes both the cultivation of crops and the domestication of animals. It is the science of farming, which is raising crops like corn, beans, peas, soybeans and also raising animals like cows, sheep, pigs, goats and chickens.

Astonishing fact

1.5 billion cups of tea are enjoyed throughout the world every day!

Food production through agriculture

Astonishing fact

To make one kilo of honey, bees have to visit 4 million flowers, travelling a distance equal to 4 times around the Earth.

As the most profound resource, agriculture provides food, clothing and shelter to us. With the spread of knowledge of the most advanced implements, there has been immense progress in the spread of agriculture, as well as agricultural output. The use of agricultural machinery, scientific methods of farming and diversification of crops have improved the overall production of agricultural crops the world over.

Agriculture is important for not only providing food but also for providing raw materials for other industries like textile, sugar, jute, vegetable oil and tobacco. Besides being an occupation for people, agriculture is also a way of living.

Most of the world's customs and cultures revolve around agriculture. A number of festivals and holidays around the world are in conjunction with reaping or harvesting or any other aspect of farming. It increases the supply of food and tax revenue to the government.

Taste of food

Taste is the sensing of flavour in food and other material that is ingested. Taste is possible because chemicals stimulate receptors on the tongue, the taste buds. How something tastes can tell an individual whether that something is food or inedible, like cardboard and toxic substances often have a disdainful taste, something that some animals and insects use to their advantage.

The four common types of taste are the basic sweet, salty, bitter and sour sensations. However, a fifth taste was recently added to the list, savoury (also known as meaty or umami).

The bumpy texture of the tongue, which is often visible, is caused by the taste buds (sometimes called **gustatory cells**). The bumps are actually called papillae and within them are microvilli, microscopic hairs that send messages to the nervous system. These nerve endings are stimulated by chemicals. The average person has thousands (approximately 10,000) of these taste receptors on their tongue and the taste that is tasted depends entirely on which chemical signal is sent.

Astonishing fact

Bananas are the world's most popular fruit after tomatoes.

Taste of food

Sweetness

Sweetness is one of the five basic tastes and is almost universally regarded as a pleasurable experience. Foods rich in simple carbohydrates such as sugar are those most commonly associated with sweetness, although there are other natural and artificial compounds that are sweet at much lower concentrations, allowing their use as non-caloric sugar substitutes.

Sweet taste is also found in milk and milk products (like butter, ghee and cream), most grains (especially wheat, rice, and barley), many legumes (like beans and lentils), sweet fruits (such as bananas and mangos) and certain cooked vegetables (such as carrots, sweet potatoes and beets).

Saltiness

Saltiness is a taste produced by the presence of sodium chloride (and to a lesser degree other salts). The ions of salt, especially sodium can pass directly through ion channels in the tongue, leading to an action potential. It is found in any salt (such as sea salt and rock salt), sea vegetables (like seaweed and kelp), and foods to which large amounts of salt are added (like nuts, chips and pickles).

> 60 million tons of tomatoes and 44 million tons of bananas are produced annually. Apples are the third most popular (36 million tons) fruit which is produced, then oranges (34 million tons) and then watermelons (22 million tons).

FOOD

Sourness

Sour is a basic taste that is considered agreeable only in small amounts. An aversive taste, it wards off the ingestion of harmful substances. It is commonly found in citrus fruits (such as lemon and limes), sour milk products (like yogurt, cheese and sour cream) and fermented substances (including wine, vinegar, pickles, sauerkraut and soy sauce).

Bitterness

Bitterness is perceived by many to be unpleasant. It is found in green leafy vegetables (such as spinach, kale and green cabbage), other vegetables (including zucchini and eggplant), herbs and spices (like turmeric, fenugreek and dandelion root), coffee, tea and certain fruits (such as grapefruits, olives, and bitter melon). While bitter taste is often not appealing alone, it stimulates the appetite and helps bring out the flavour of the other tastes.

Savouriness (Umami)

Umami is a Japanese word meaning 'savoury' or 'meaty' and thus applies to

the sensation of savouriness. Umami is an appetitive taste facilitating ingestion of protein-rich food and it is variously described as a savoury, brothy or meaty taste. Umami can be tasted in cheese and soy sauce and while also found in many other fermented and aged foods this taste is also present in tomatoes, grains and beans.

Astonishing fact

There are more than 10,000 varieties of tomatoes!

Methods of preparing food

Baking

Baking is simply a cooking technique in which dry heat is applied to a food product in a closed environment, such as an oven. During the baking process, consistent temperature is maintained to ensure proper browning and doneness.

Baking is one of the most versatile of cooking techniques because it can achieve a variety of unique results-puffy soufflés, crispy baked potatoes, creamy casseroles and delicate pastries-using one simple but exacting method. Put together your ingredients in the right proportions, select the appropriate oven temperature and maintain that temperature consistently throughout the baking process and your finished result should be perfect.

Astonishing fact
The can opener was invented 48 years after cans were introduced.

Barbecuing

Nothing beats the deep, rich flavour of good barbecue. Barbecue refers to the slow, indirect cooking of meats over a wood, charcoal or gas flame. The meat is often seasoned with rubs, sauces or mops. This same method is known as barbie in Australia and braai in South Africa. Asian barbecue on the other hand, uses thinly sliced meat and seafood, often highly seasoned, that is quick-cooked on a hot grill or a searing hotplate.

FOOD

Braising

Braising is a form of moist-heat cooking in which the item to be cooked is partially covered with liquid and then simmered slowly at a low temperature. Braising is a good way to cook the tougher cuts of meat such as shank, shoulder and round. Long, slow simmering breaks down the connective tissue in the meat. However, delicate foods such as fish and seafood can also be braised. Cooking time is simply shorter.

The liquid used as a braising medium is usually water or stock, but wine, beer or tomatoes are sometimes used. And other ingredients such and onions, carrots or potatoes are often added to impart different flavours.

Astonishing fact
Over the last 40 years food production actually increased faster than population.

Frying

Frying is the cooking of food with oil. Due to the higher temperature of oil compared with water-based cooking, the cooking time is much shorter.

Deep frying is a frying process where the food is completely immersed in oil. Stir frying is a way of quick cooking foods with a small amount of oil over high heat. This ingenious cooking method from the East preserves the flavour, freshness and nutrients of a dish's ingredients. Since cooking goes so quickly, the main thing to remember when stir frying is to have all your ingredients prepared and close at hand before you begin cooking.

Methods of preparing food

Astonishing fact
In the Middle Ages, sugar was a treasured luxury costing 9 times as much as milk.

Grilling

Grilling is the quick cooking of meat, fish or vegetables over intense heat. It is a form of cooking that involves dry heat applied to the surface of food, commonly from above or below. Grilling usually involves quite a lot of direct, radiant heat and tends to be used for cooking quickly meat that has already been cut into slices. Food to be grilled is cooked on a grill (an open wire grid with a heat source above or below), a grill pan (similar to a frying pan, but with raised ridges to mimic the wires of an open grill) or griddle (a flat plate heated from below).

Items to be grilled can be flavoured in a marinade or seasoned with a rub (a type of marinade-wet or dry). They can be basted while cooking with any variety of flavourful sauces, or topped with a flavoured butter before serving.

Poaching

Poaching is a great way of cooking food that cuts fat, enhances flavour and keeps delicate foods from turning tough. This simple cooking method involves slow simmering eggs, meat, poultry, fish, seafood or fruit in a flavourful liquid just long enough to cook it through.

FOOD

Astonishing fact
Approximately one billion snails are served in restaurants annually.

Preserving

In days before the refrigerator, the only way to get food to last through lean times was through various methods of preservation. Drying, curing, brining, pickling, fermenting and smoking are just some of the ways used for preserving food. These methods have all survived modernization simply because they make food so tasty.

Roasting

With roasting, direct heat is applied to the food. The heat seals the outside part of the food and the juice inside the food cooks the food. Roasting is mainly used when cooking fleshy food like fish, meat or chicken. When heat is applied to the outer covering of the food, it seals it up thereby trapping all the juices inside the food. The action of direct heating, heats up the juices inside the food, which then cooks the food. Again there is very little nutrient lost and the flavour is not spoilt. Food is frequently rotated over the spit so that there is even heating applied to all parts of the food. This is done so that heat is applied evenly to the food to make it get cooked properly.

Methods of preparing food

Sautéing

Sautéing is a form of cooking that uses a very hot pan and a small amount of fat to cook the food very quickly. Sautéing browns the food's surface as it cooks and develops complex flavours and aromas. It generally consists of searing portion-sized cuts of meat or fish in hot oil on both sides to brown. The meat or fish is then removed, and the remaining bits and juices in the pan are incorporated into either a pre-made sauce or the sauce is made directly in the pan.

Steaming

Steaming involves suspending food over simmering or boiling water and cooking it with the resulting steam. Steaming as a method is valued for the fact that it preserves vitamins and minerals in the food that might otherwise be washed away with boiling. It is also a way to cut back on fat, since none is needed.

Astonishing fact

Tea is said to have been discovered in 2737 BC by a Chinese emperor when some tea leaves accidentally blew into a pot of boiling water.

The simplest way to steam food is to place a steaming basket in a saucepan over about an inch or two of water. Place the food to be steamed in the basket, cover it with a lid and bring the water to a slow boil. Most foods will finish cooking in anywhere from 5 to 10 minutes.

Many vegetables are ideal for steaming, as are fillets of fish and many types of shellfish. Tougher cuts of meat are not as good for steaming since they need more cooking time to get tender. But chicken breasts do well.

FOOD

> ### Astonishing fact
> An onion, apple and potato all have the same taste. The differences in flavour are caused by their smell.

Stewing

When chunks of meat, seafood or vegetables are slow-simmered in a flavourful liquid brew, the result is a warming, comforting dish called a stew. Slow, moist cooking is the best way to tenderize tough cuts of meat. Stews are also a great way to use up leftovers.

In the stewing method food is cooked using a lot of liquid. Different kinds of vegetables are chopped, diced or cubed and added to the pot. Sometimes pieces of selected meat, fish or chicken is also chopped and added to the stew. The liquid is slightly thickened and stewed food is served in that manner. This method is also used when preparing fruits that are going to be served as desserts. With this cooking method, every food is cooked together at the same time in one pot. The flavour, colours, shapes and textures of the different vegetables that are used, makes stewing a handy method of cooking.

Boiling

This is the most common method of cooking and is also the simplest. With this method of cooking, enough water is added to food and it is then cooked over the fire. The action of the heated water makes the food to get cooked. The liquid is usually thrown away after the food is cooked. In the case of cooking rice, all the water is absorbed by the rice grains to get it cooked. During the heating process, the nutrients can get lost or destroyed and the flavour can be reduced with this method of cooking.

Food trade

Food is now traded on a global basis. The variety and availability of food is no longer restricted by the diversity of locally grown food or the limitations of the local growing season. Between 1961 and 1999 there has been a 400 per cent increase in worldwide food exports. Some countries are now economically dependent on food exports, which in some cases account for over 80 per cent of all exports.

Food is an essential part of our lives, which is why the way it is grown, processed and transported is worth understanding and improving. Broadly, the food industry comprises a complex network of activities pertaining to the supply, consumption and catering of food products and services across the world. Finished food products and partially prepared 'instant' food packets are also a part of the food industry. The food industry employs a massive number of skilled and unskilled workers. In 2006 alone, the food industry accounted for over 1.5 million jobs in the US and 4 million jobs in Europe.

A number of factors heighten the demand in the global food industry such as the population levels, wealth distribution, health awareness (organic food) and types of varied lifestyles. The people responsible for the food supply take many things into account like the quality of the supply chain, level of competition in the industry and the composition of the target consumers.

The world's first chocolate candy was produced in 1828 by Dutch chocolate-maker Conrad J. Van Houten.

Food poverty

Food poverty can be defined as the 'inability to obtain healthy affordable food'. This maybe because people lack shops in their area or have trouble reaching them. Other factors influencing food access are the availability of a range of healthy goods in local shops, income, transport, fear of crime, knowledge about what constitutes a healthy diet and the skills to create healthy meals.

Due to this complex mix of factors, people on low incomes have the lowest intakes of fruit and vegetables and are far more likely to suffer from diet-related diseases such as cancer, diabetes, obesity and coronary heart disease. Food poverty can also be about an overabundance of 'junk' food as well as a lack of healthy food.

Households in food poverty do not have enough food to meet the energy and nutrient needs of all of their members. Depending on patterns of food distribution within a household at least one member of a food-poor household is always hungry but, potentially, all members are.

Some households live under conditions of chronic or seasonal food poverty. Other households are pushed into food poverty because of changes in area food availability and/or in their own ability to secure entitlement to food.

Astonishing fact

There are more than 100 varieties of thyme.

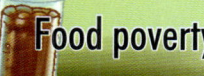

Food poverty

The first volume of recipes was published in 62 A.D. by the Roman Apicius. Titled De Re Coquinaria, it described the feasts enjoyed by the Emperor Claudius.

About 25,000 people die every day of hunger or hunger-related causes, according to the United Nations. Unfortunately, it is children who die most often.

Yet there is plenty of food in the world for everyone. The problem is that hungry people are trapped in severe poverty. They lack the money to buy enough food to nourish themselves. Being constantly malnourished, they become weaker and often sick. This makes them increasingly less able to work, which then makes them even poorer and hungrier. This downward spiral often continues until death occurs for them and their families.

There are effective programs to break this spiral. For adults, there are 'food for work' programs where the adults are paid with food to build schools, dig wells, make roads, etc. This does both— nourishes them and builds infrastructure to end the poverty. For children, there are 'food for education' programs where the children are provided with food when they attend school. Their education will help them to escape from hunger and global poverty.

Food allergy and intolerance

A **food allergy** is a term that health experts reserve for any abnormal reaction by the body's disease-fighting immune system to an otherwise harmless food or component of food.

When a reaction to a food occurs that does not involve the body's immune system, it is called food intolerance. This is not a food allergy.

Food intolerance stems from problems with digestion or metabolism. Usually the problem involves a defect or deficiency in an enzyme in the body, a chemical necessary for the breakdown or absorption of a particular food deficiency.

Food allergies occur when the immune system attacks certain proteins in certain foods. The substances in the food that trigger this immune-system response, are called **allergens**.

The immune system is a complex network of cells and molecules that help defend the body against foreign substances. When a properly functioning immune system detects a foreign substance, it responds to this threat by producing proteins called antibodies against the invaders. The antibodies will recognize and attack this foreign substance when they next encounter it. This 'battle' is what causes the allergy symptoms.

Typical symptoms of food allergy includes, swelling of face, lips and tongue, hives, dizziness, breathlessness, tingling sensation or fainting. In general, food allergy is experienced by 2 per cent of adults and 6 per cent of children. The most common food allergies are peanuts, tree nuts (such as walnuts, pecans and almonds), fish and shellfish, milk, eggs, soy products and wheat.

Astonishing fact

When ketchup was originally developed by the Chinese in 1690, it contained no tomatoes. It was made out of pickled fish, shellfish and spices.

Food allergy and intolerance

Food intolerance is a digestive system response rather than an immune system response. It occurs when something in a food irritates a person's digestive system or when a person is unable to properly digest or breakdown the food. Intolerance to lactose, which is found in milk and other dairy products is the most common food intolerance.

Lactose intolerance is the most common type of food intolerance experienced by many. Enzyme lactase is deficient in such individuals. Lactase is essential for lactose (milk sugar) breakdown in milk and milk products. Symptoms of lactose intolerance include bloating, diarrhoea, abdominal discomfort and gas. Differentiating food intolerance from food allergy is important to prevent recurrence. Food allergies fail to allow even a miniscule amount of the food, whereas, small portions of the particular food can be eaten in case of food intolerance.

There are many factors that may contribute to food intolerance. In some cases, as with lactose intolerance, the person lacks the chemicals called enzymes necessary to properly digest certain proteins found in food. Also common are intolerances to some chemical ingredients added to food to provide colour, enhance taste, and protect against the growth of bacteria.

Astonishing fact

In South Africa, termites are often roasted and eaten by the handful like popcorn!

FOOD

Food allergies affect about 2 to 4 per cent of adults and 6 to 8 per cent of children. Food intolerances are much more common. In fact, nearly everyone at one time has had an unpleasant reaction to something they ate. Some people have specific food intolerances.

Food allergies can be triggered by even a small amount of the food and occur every time the food is consumed. People with food allergies are generally advised to avoid the offending foods completely. On the other hand, food intolerances often are dose related.

People with food intolerance may not have symptoms unless they eat a large portion of the food or eat the food frequently. For example, a person with lactose intolerance maybe able to drink milk in coffee or a single glass of milk, but becomes sick if he or she drinks several glasses of milk.

Food allergies and intolerances are also different from food poisoning, which generally results from spoiled or tainted food and affects more than one person eating the food.

India is the world's largest producer of turmeric powder as well as the world's largest consumer of the powder.

Food safety methods

Food safety is the utilization of various resources and strategies to ensure that all types of foods are properly stored, prepared and preserved so they are safe for consumption. Practicing this level of food sanitation begins with the purchase or acquisition of different food items and ends with the proper storage of leftovers for future use. Many of the food safety methods used in restaurants can also be employed at home. Here are some examples.

One of the most important aspects of practicing food safety involves preventing foods from becoming contaminated. Making sure foods are stored properly goes a long way in avoiding any type of food contamination. Meat and vegetables should be placed in airtight containers and placed in a freezer. Items such as flour, sugar, cornmeal and spices should also be stored in containers that provide an effective barrier to airborne bacteria, and can be stored in pantries when not in active use.

Basic kitchen sanitation guidelines are also an important component of any food safety strategy. Preparation counters should be disinfected regularly. Cutting boards should also be cleaned after each use. Knives, spatulas, pans, pots and other tools used in the preparation of food should be washed in hot soapy water or run through a dishwasher. This can help minimize the opportunity for food residue to breed bacteria that could contaminate food the next time the tools are used.

Astonishing fact

There are more than 500 avocado varieties.

Care should also be taken to wash all fresh fruits and vegetables thoroughly before initiating any type of food preparation. This simple process will help remove a significant amount of germs and bacteria reducing the chances of some type of food borne illness from developing. With foods that are peeled, washing helps to prevent the transfer of contaminants from the peel to the knife and ultimately to the food itself.

Leftovers should be placed in airtight containers and placed into the refrigerator or freezer immediately after a meal. This helps to preserve the leftovers for use in other dishes at a later date by maintaining the quality of the food and protecting it from possible contamination. Doing so makes it possible to utilize leftover corn, potatoes and other vegetables in soups or casseroles at a later date, with no worries about possible contamination.

Practicing food safety not only helps to maintain good health, but can also help save money. Storing food properly, as well as making sure to prepare food in a clean environment, means that there is less chance of food spoiling and being thrown out.

Unsafe food causes many acute and life-long diseases, ranging from diarrhoeal diseases to various forms of cancer. WHO estimates that food borne and waterborne diarrhoeal diseases taken together kill about 2.2 million people annually.

Astonishing fact

Archaeologists have evidence of people eating apples as far back as 6500 B.C.

Test Your MEMORY

1. What is food?

2. Name the types of food.

3. Name the food sources.

4. What is a food chain?

5. Write briefly about food production through agriculture.

6. What are the different tastes of food?

7. What are the various methods for the preparation of food?

8. What is food trade?

9. What is food poverty?

10. What is food allergy?

11. What is food intolerance?

12. Write some food safety methods.

FOOD

Index

A
agriculture 3, 12, 13
allergens 26
antibodies 26

B
baking 17
barbecuing 17
bitter 14, 16
boiling 21, 22
braising 18

C
carnivores 10, 11

D
decomposers 10, 11
deep frying 18

E
ecology 10
ecosystem 10

F
fast food 4, 5
fibre 6
food allergy 26, 27
food chain 10, 11
food intolerance 26, 27
food poisoning 28
food poverty 24
food safety 3, 29, 30
food science 3

fruits 4, 6, 7, 8, 15, 16, 22, 30
frying 18, 19

G
grilling 19

H
herbivores 10, 11

I
immune system 26, 27

J
junk food 5, 24

L
lactose intolerance 27, 28

M
minerals 5, 6, 21

N
nutrition 3

O
obesity 5, 6, 24
organic food 7, 23

P
poaching 19
preserving 20
primary 10, 11
primary consumers 10

processing 6
producers 10, 11

R
refinement 6
roasting 20

S
salty 14
sautéing 21
secondary consumers 10, 11
sour 14, 16
steaming 21
stewing 22
stir frying 18
sweet 14, 15

T
taste 14, 15, 16, 22, 27
taste buds 14

U
umami 14, 16

V
vegetables 4, 6, 7, 8, 15, 16, 19, 21, 22, 24, 29, 30
vitamins 5, 6, 21

W
water 3, 6, 9, 18, 21, 22, 29
whole foods 6